Noon until Night

Richard Hoffman

Noon until Night

Richard Hoffman

Barrow Street Press
New York City

Designed by Robert Drummond
Cover painting by Steve Klarer,
  Sitting Guy with the Blues
Author photo by Barbara Trachtenberg

Published 2016 by Barrow Street, Inc., a not-for-profit
(501) (c) 3) corporation. All contributions are tax deductible.
Distributed by:
  Barrow Street Books
  P.O. Box 1558
  Kingston, RI 02881

Barrow Street Books are also distributed by Small Press Distribution,
SPD, 1341 Seventh Street Berkeley, CA 94710-1409, spd@spdbooks.org;
(510) 524-1668, (800) 869-7553 (Toll-free within the US); amazon.com;
Ingram Periodicals Inc., 1240 Heil Quaker Blvd, PO Box 7000,
La Vergne TN 37086-700 (615) 213-3574; and Armadillo & Co.,
7310 S. La Cienega Blvd, Inglewood, CA 90302, (310) 693-6061.

Special thanks to the University of Rhode Island English Department
and especially the PhD Program in English, 60 Upper College Road,
Swan 114, Kingston, RI 02881, (401) 874-5931, which provides
valuable in-kind support, including graduate and undergraduate interns.

First Edition

Library of Congress Control Number: 2016961009

ISBN 978-0-9973184-4-9

for Kathi, as always

CONTENTS

Envoi from a Headland

No farther; no turning back:
        here at the verge hold out
                your crisscrossed palm.

Honor my dead, if not in words,
        then in their incorporeal,
                represented breathing.

Let go the reappearing faces
        down the generations. Speak
                in the urgent voices

I am able to hear sometimes
        in silences, familiar noises,
                and the sound of rain.

Inside, let the broken
        halves be not opposed,
                neither Janus nor Narcissus,

but angled, mirrors
        to see around corners,
                over walls, to look far down

below the lip of the cliff
        at jagged rocks, the suck and
                boom, moil, hiss, and foam.

Part One

Whoever You Are

In every age are two people
charged with holding up the sky.

Those who know them know
something's different about them.

Usually, the two do not meet;
however, sometimes, after eons,

the law of averages requires
they collide, transforming both.

Those two were your parents.
But you knew that, didn't you?

Patrimony

1.

He is out of work.
We are out of money.
My mother's patience
makes him feel worse.
He has lost his temper
again and he is sorry.

Priests have told him
ever since he was a boy
to stop touching himself.
He hides the magazines,
thinks himself weak.

In the doorway of a plane,
you jump, you do not
shake and shit yourself,
kicked into the flak-lit
night the stench of you
like a thing already dead.
It is a long way down.
A lot can go wrong, so
he pretends to know
what a man is, and death;
nothing under his feet
as percussive waves
of light explode around him
like shots of whiskey.

Later he makes believe
he is still the man he
can't remember, the boy
he can't remember.
Maybe there is another
story he was to live.

Maybe he was lazy
and missed his chance.

He wants to be the man
he imagines his wife
loves, the god his father
was to him, the god
he hopes his sons think
him. Complexion: "Ruddy,"
it says on his license.
A doctor diagnoses him
with hypertension.
He loves but still believes
he is pretending.

2.

A son might hold a father
to account for certain
memories, for certain
understandings, to desire
anyone, or anything at all.
A lot can go wrong, so
he pretends to know
what a man is, and love.
He may have to help himself

to his father's shame
for a time to understand.
Sometimes a long time.
And then, even if he turns,
if he rises and bathes
and dresses and shaves
and takes up his life at last,
he cannot say if that is
or is not forgiveness.

The much he must learn
becomes his fate. There is
no might have been, no
otherwise or *if only,* only
the ground under his feet.

Elsewhere men continue
falling from the sky.

A Face in the Ceiling

In August heat, I am remembering my father.
"Stinkin' hot," he would have called this day,
his T-shirt wet with sweat over his heart, wet
circles under his arms, dark patch between his
shoulder blades. I am remembering my father,
a year now since his death has scattered him,
no longer all in one place anymore, no longer
in one time. Now, piecing him back together

near the anniversary of his dissolution,
questions — not coming from me, not curiosity
but necessity (mine and his together) — form
in the discontinuous and widening vacancies
of memory, questions like sweat, beading
on my forehead. This is work, not to let him go,
not yet, and to ask if I have understood him;
hazardous work. I am remembering my father

as he was in my earliest memories, home
from "the steel" where he laid track in the yards,
sprawled on the floor of the living room, spent,
in his boxer shorts in front of an oscillating fan
that dinged at intervals at some point in its sweep
(I swear I can hear it now. I can hear it!).
I lay next to him, and he asked if I could see
the faces in the cracked and water-stained ceiling.

Yes. I saw them there. Who were they? But
by then he was asleep, so I pretended I was too.
One time at least, I was. Some years later, home
from his job with the city, ("Those years," he'd say,
"I was with the city") a restaurant inspector,
("protecting the public," he'd say and roll his eyes)
in the same blue uniform as a cop, without the gun,
I spied on him searching his face in the mirror.

For what? For whom? I am remembering my father
with the help of photographs and a single video
in which he says how good it feels to tell the truth.
You have to think of a man in time, even a father.
I think of him as a man on whom lies were heaped
until he could hardly breathe. I think that goodness
prior to injury is innocence, and that goodness after
injury is courage. I am remembering my father.

The Wave

How does a swell become a wave?
What pushes up from under water?
Tell me; this tired body is all I have

become of all I tried to be; I move
more slowly now and wonder:
how does a swell become a wave?

There isn't much I wouldn't give
for strength and will to rise together
in this tired body, but if all I have

is this one heavy life, then let me heave
it, somehow, all of it, into the future,
the way a swell becomes a wave

that rolls for miles to a beach or cove
or thunders on rock and shatters.
I am tired of this tired body. All I have

to live for — my children, others I love —
I'm too fatigued for them to matter.
How does a swell become a wave?
Tell me! This tired body is all I have.

Photo

Pregnant, my mother
in brilliant sunlight:

I must have known
even then this serene

vermilion, this blind
and bloody forgiveness.

Infant

You begin with your mother's eyes
gazing on the wordlessness of you,
her eyes where you see trees, a forest
of consequences deep into distance

and ruins and fire and the billion
hues of sunrise, and even the dark
is her. You need not fear although
the stars are trembling on that water,

tired from their long journey, and
that feeling of breaking, falling,
will remain and from time to time
become available again, her eyes

the whole of the story then, of you:
torn from her tired body, rooted
in her troubled, earnest mind,
no knowledge yet of your fortune.

Shoes

My mother cut holes in her shoes
so her corns would stick out, not
torment her, standing all day
in a mill folding woolen sweaters.

Her shoes stank. They were ugly.
Twin lobsters in a tank at the market,
laces defeated antennae, children
tapping at the glass, saying, "Eww."

And she cut linoleum to cover,
from inside, the holes in the soles
because those were the only shoes
she could bear to wear to work

and because she needed to work.
And she soaked her feet in the evening
and smoked and listened to the radio
and imagined walking — where?

Good Boy

His mother's
chapped lips, flecks
of Lucky
she said *thpt, thpt*
to be rid of,

he cracked, bled
without warning,
held back words,
made himself
a zero,
a portal for smoke.

All That First Chapter

1949. The smoke had cleared and the radiation
went wherever it goes and people went

wherever they decided forward was and I,
firstborn, took the usual year or so

to establish a self behind my eyes
to spend the next half-century wanting

all of it, from the chestnut trees
to the gravel, to small shards of coal left

glittering after a delivery, slugs and salamanders
under lifted slabs of slate, anthills

and honeybees in clover asterisked
with dandelions in the tiny yard

while Mother sang in the kitchen, tunes
from the radio and Tin Pan Alley,

and before I learned to pretend or dissemble,
I hurt myself to make her run to me.

Mondays were sailing with sheets, curtains,
the world past grief, through the wringer,

prosperity, good washing weather.
I learned to read before I started school,

mother-tongue feeding me, birdlike,
a *Little Golden Book* from the A&P, or pasting

S&H Green Stamps into a booklet of squares
carefully, filthy fingers learning joy

could be had just sitting in a chair,
trying to get a thing right and be praised;

brachiating neurons chemically articulated
the future. The church was the past

and Europe. My parents knelt; I thought
how God had given us twenty-six letters,

and I had learned them, and could
make them all, but weren't there more?

I thought I could see a few others
in the moving net of liquid light reflected

on the hull of an aluminum canoe,
already a sinner, as miserable with desire

as our neighbor's dog leashed to a tree,
barking and straining, that taut rope

the radius of his disdain. The houses
on our the street were one long structure

like an egg crate or ice tray: behind
each door a father home from the war,

and now another, (our paperboy there,
wounded, his picture in the paper.)

I delivered the news too, folding and
tucking it just so to make an oblong

aerodynamic package that hit the door
and opened, a headline for the just-awakened

I'd imagined as I packed in darkness.
I spent my earnings on books to help me

say good-bye, to want to say good-bye,
and boarded the bus, transistor in my ear.

Watching

Because I lay on my back as a boy
in the grass of the small yard behind our house

        watching clouds move and become
                            faces, mostly,

I was able to sit for a long time
        holding my dying mother's hand
                as her sleeping face changed
        like a field in the sun
under drifting
                    clouds,

and hold my newborn grandson,
        his features changing
moment to moment,
                      affected by something
        perhaps like dreaming

at which I wonder.

An American Boyhood

My toy gun looked just like the gun my father carried in the war. It looked like the guns on TV. I learned to make the sound of gunfire with my mouth. No one made the sound of a ricocheting bullet better: a loud plosive followed by a little whistle, diminuendo. I spent a lot of time in my fantasy world, drawing on bad guys, pivoting and crouching. I holstered my gun. Drew it again. When I got bored, I sat on a swing and wondered where everybody else was. I did all these things. If you had an American boyhood, so did you. Tamir Rice had an American boyhood; his was a black one, a short one.

A Story

I opened the book
and a thin slip
of paper, nothing
on it, twirled
and fluttered to the floor.

Look! said the boy,
my grandson, twisting from
my lap to retrieve it.
Can I have it?
Can I keep it? Please?

Sufferance

Rain, rain, go on,

rain. I've been given
this time by my mother.
I've known about water
forever, and fear
is no stranger either.

Rain. Go on. Rain.
The fires burn

no matter what I do,
the fires of my fathers,
and will sear me
one day, maybe soon,
and also you.

Burn, go on and burn.
We are not much —

light, ash, particulate
of the erotic and such
temporary tragedies
as interrupt it. To call us
seeds would serve,

or waterbeads, or sparks.
Go on. On and on.

Part Two

Noon until Night

"per entro i luoghi tristi
venni stamane, e sono in prima vita,
ancor che l'altra, sì andando, acquisti."
Dante, *Purgatorio*, Canto VIII, l.58-60

"by way of the regions of sorrow
I came this morning, and I am still in my
first life, seeking another with this journey."
tr. W. S. Merwin

Even were I the sun I knew that I would be afraid
from dawn to noon that I would never make it
and from noon until night that I might die;

and no one knew I was afraid because I was afraid
of what would happen if I let them see. No way
to live I told myself, no way to think about living,

and yet, were it not for my fear, I would have gone
too far; I would have passed the narrow gate where
ideas of sin and mercy, fabricated to appear as natural,

hide the one real reason to go on, the original one
the birds articulate their several ways each morning,
implicit in their leading question: Is it you? Is it you?

One of us is going to have to rise and set out, then,
with no assurance of arrival, nor of any welcome
if we make it there where we have guessed the new to be,

just like the old days, in leaky boats, through storms
toward a hunch, toward what we've been told of by others
whose credibility is vouched for only by their scars

and the cohesion and agreement of their stories, though
we know they're not beyond a bit of fun at our expense
and always want to be remunerated for intelligence,

so we have to weigh, still, the tone, the spirit if you will,
with which a course is offered to us; at the same time
we have everything to lose, friends, and no time to waste.

Whenever you're given a choice between two options
be suspicious. Hands, feet, eyes, ears, wings, all come
in twos; most twos are pairs, not opposites; couples,

not competitors. That we have had to learn this
means there are many unexamined lies bequeathed
us all that only serve the ends of some, and it is

even harder for the ones who benefit to see it.
Look: would you rather keep the things you have
or live like those desolate people on the screen?

This looks like a forest, but every tree was planted.
The opposite of magic is discouragement, not logic.
To the disenchanted, any third thing calls adventure.

Euclidian space can only handle three coordinates,
like us. At any given moment, in 3-D, life invites
us, hungry and dressed in our best reds and greens,

while colorless time, which doesn't make a fuss,
first loves and nurtures and then, without permission,
undoes us. At least if we're lucky and long-lasting.

If this is an illusion, a tickling of rods and cones,
then I should hollow an ancestor's bone and measure
a hole for each finger at the sweetest space apart

and labor to make a music that might reconcile
the three dimensions with my foursquare heart,
summoning words from north, south, east, and west.

Cadence of the highway's seams beneath my tires,
I hear it in 4/4 time. Dithyramb-badam-badam-badam.
It's an old road I'm on. An old road in need of repairs.

It doesn't go everywhere. The boy who thought it did,
who thought it would for him, was young, not wrong.
One morning, though I don't remember, I must have

tired of my four white walls' oblivion, their gallery
of martyrs left by the previous tenant. I straightened them,
could never bring myself to take them down. Again,

I had no name for the knowledge that moved me then,
that signaled — was it I who set that alarm? When? —
the time had arrived, as appointed, to come to my senses.

A fifth of whiskey a day's no way to look for anything;
oblivion, maybe, but after a while not even reliably that.
The wind was kicking up and I luffed, not anybody's sail,

not even mine, but a sheet hung on a backyard clothesline
by my mother long ago, still threatening to come loose
from the wooden clothespins painted to look like people

and rise, bright and tumbling, as if it were finally free,
the air embodied, grace and dynamism made articulate,
the dream, bright white, of being no one, last conceit

of the defeated some have made philosophy, idea
that one choicelessness is better than the other. Six feet
below this agon, my dead revised their view, released me.

So grievous losses find their place, and mourning ends
like a mismatched love. I wish someone had told me,
though I wouldn't have believed it; how could anyone

convince me I would hardly remember their names,
never mind their gestures, their gait, their loveliness.
That had they lived we might have found ourselves

estranged is something I can comprehend, but only
now when I no longer need such shrugging comfort,
now when longevity itself begins to seem at once

the only wealth worth having and the booby prize.
If every seven years our bodies are refurbished,
every cell regenerated, why do I not feel restored?

And all through those changes the same deadly sins,
the same temptations and senseless worries the only
future visible at all, the sad dream of a wonkish monk,

the best a wan penurious erotophobe in love
with dismal numerology could do. I ought to know;
I shrugged and took the via negativa through

a plenitude gone rank and sour and unappealing
(then bragged I had resisted the forbidden fruit.)
When I tired of saying I am not this, I am not that,

all the signs — of dreams, of coincidence, of confluence
— meant that from here on only hope held any hope
of wisdom. Early moonrise. Eight bells. Nightfall,

with August's furious insect mantras a kind
of hypnagogic endless present, as if each creature,
intricate and brittle, heartsick in the pitiless dark,

was screaming in the only way it had been given,
with the only hard-shelled body that it had, an
incomprehensible earnest need that may be what we

sound like to the heavens if listeners are out there.
Or are they answering each to each? (I hope they are.)
Or are we all one cry, a prayer, a plume of sound

spinning off the earth like a comet's tail, returning
echo of a wounded emptiness's outraged initiation,
all nine phyla in chorus? Plus this one imagined voice.

Like a child I do not want to go to sleep. Like a man
in the ICU I am afraid to close my eyes. Like a woman
at last in labor later than the calendar foretold, I am

adjacent the unknowable and feeling I am falling from
a crenel in a wall, sentry of a singular illustration, into
a turbulent darkness. Could it be that nothing further

is required but my assent? Why clench, clamp, tense,
clutch, hold? I have not loved enough, not nearly.
How many of my struggles have I chosen not to know

I've chosen? Which ones have spelled my name to those
I leave behind? I've only learned I would be wise
to count to ten before I speak, perhaps not even then.

Had I known how little was in my hands, how long
I had been tumbling toward this darkness, I could not
have stood that understanding. It seemed to weigh

so much, require such constancy. (Now all at once I see
this poem is a good-bye. It frightens me.) I have returned
where vanishing is possible, this time for real, my earlier

dread rehearsal. I know nothing of tides and even less
of stars, nor of the seasons: what to plant and when.
I have not had to. Or so I thought. This fear is different:

that this bound life which tired me so was all imagined
or misunderstood. Who lied to me? Why? To whose
advantage? Who can bear to ask at the eleventh hour?

Fast to this crux, drawn at this junction where time is
quartered, I no longer think it courageous to live
with neither God's nor the world's consolations,

only necessary. And I no longer give much to Caesar
either, if I can help it. Laughter I distrust — it is so close
to forgetting — but I laugh despite myself, and cry

sometimes with neither clear cause nor resistance.
How can I say this? How can this be said? Yes,
I would live it all again, unchanged, although

I seldom knew that I was happy. I fold my hands,
so differently gifted, one on the other, close my eyes,
consent to being one ring on the river in unending rain.

Part Three

For a Slain Poet

Your killers drew the zipper across the black bag like
the sign friends made across their mouths
when you opened yours in the wrong company

                    and carried you out of there.

Kings, we all know, build palaces,
hoard riches, gather armies of impoverished
and fierce young men, and make war.

But a king who will kill a poet out of fear?
There remains no evil on earth he will not do.

You, however, who have reminded us
of the truth of the lovers we are, you are
already in paradise

where, solely for your pleasure,
the one god has bestowed upon you twenty-seven
blank pages
and your favorite pen,

along with a whole new alphabet
made from the shadows of birds in flight,

the flash of ripples on the lake in sunlight,

letters in the shapes of the many intersecting shadows of the grass,

and the sheen of blown sand, sheared from the crest
of a shifting dune by the Khamaseen,

marks to represent the sound of weeping,
signs for the sound of laughter,

but nothing too clear, none of them
just right, nowhere the once-and-for-all expression

that would obliterate desire. If I thought
what you wanted was rest, if any of your poems
could be so construed, I would wish you rest.

Of Thee

My country wonders at the looks it gets.
It likes to hang around the Army/Navy store,
admiring this uniform and that insignia,
badges and big blocky numbers for everyone,
singing "Take Me Out to the Ballgame" off-key.
It is always looking in the gutters for money.
With a gun from its collection, it shot itself
right smack in the history. It can't remember.
Something's been stolen but it can't say what.
It can't remember, so everything happens now.
It likes to hang around the Army/Navy store,
admiring this uniform and that insignia,
badges and big blocky numbers for everyone,
singing "Take Me Out to the Ballgame" off-key.

At CVS: Aisle 4, Magazines

Some people paid some other people
some money to write some things so that
some other people would pay some money
to read what those people wrote so that

the people who had paid for the people
to write those things would be paid back
with interest so they'd have more money
to pay new people to write the same things;

so naturally as time went on some words,
the names of some other things, vanished,
and, little by little, but accelerating, those
things the unbought words referred to

died, and what was called reading finally
became a bright and vacuumed place where
censorship was unheard of, and everyone
read whatever people were paid to write.

Glimpse and Rumor

See them before the door
closes, doing their jobs:
papers to sign, making
laws making money.
Changing the names
of streets, buildings, bridges.
Writing plausible tales. Quick
before the door closes.

Word is he's back,
baptized in our amnesia.
Cain. Cain. Wasn't he
one of Eve's boys?
Which is his cubicle?
Could be a good man
to know sometime.

Here He Comes

with his muscle, his stick,
his whistle and shtick,

his halberd, harquebus,
crucifix and mace,

his beads and rumors,
strong convictions, his

night goggles and self-portraiture.
He has a job for you, your

death and other talking points,
and your mob is no problemo

with their Maynard G. Krebs tinfoil
hearts, their scavenging and too late

willowy midnight moonrise,
not with his eyelashes

and bibliography, oh no, nor
his businesslike perversions

and his ticket to the counterfeit,
his seedless fruits and hydroponics,

along with his loud confederates,
their threatened flash and aftermath,

his endgame begun in utero, so
suddenly carnal in nomine domini

you can't believe your eyes.

Tsunami

                    Were these people

small

                            as our apathy sees them,

they might have sheltered in a cowrie shell

             or under a tern's wing;

were they all, those

                 dead,

                          as swift as our forgetting,

they would be

On Being Asked to Write a Poem on the Theme of Liberation

I wish I understood what liberation is,
but history seems to come down to this:
behind us cut sod and a mound of soil,

a trench of jerky and bone, each skull
stained and broken, an empty husk.
Our truck gasps and grinds as dusk

shifts day's hoarse gears a second time,
a dismal sound that will forever rhyme
with respite but never catharsis.

I wish I understood what liberation is.
I looked for something I could quote,
but Ecclesiastes reads like a suicide note,

and cheap grace, as the martyred Pastor
Bonhoeffer called it, that instant Easter
resurrecting victims and perps alike,

is our most cowardly mistake:
after such knowledge, what? What?
Don't. Don't speak the word. To liberate

our children's children's children,
maybe, provide them with an antigen
of an idea, maybe we can manage that

if we begin right now to search for it,
no salve, but a vaccine against malice,
so they might know what liberation is.

Pax Humana

The party's in a sweaty walk-up,
with little plates of hummus, pita,
crackers, cheese, and half a dozen kinds
of olives: green and purple and black;
salty, sour, oily, with garlic,
hot peppers, pimientos. Olives
from Greece, Sicily, Palestine,
Israel, Syria, the Azores, Italy,
shipped for a price agreed upon
against the background of the news:
who's firing rockets across whose
borders, who's now in a civil war,
who threatens and who threatens
retaliation. What peace there is,
including the people dancing here
in the center of the room to the song
a captive in a strange land sings,
arrives in one place, not another,
with olives packed in brine or oil.
On the big board or smartphone,
an algorithm, updates in real time,
adjusts to keep the dance floor level.
Marley soothes from the bookshelf
speakers: *Every ting gonna be all right*.
And little clay dishes, hand-painted
folk-art birds and vines, for the pits.

A Scar. A Fear. A War. An Ear.

Back when the scar was becoming,
back when the cut, back when
no one can remember, then
(we've been assured by countless
generations) a perfection was.
You may believe it, may even
know a story of the hand and blade,
and whose, and music with it,
but the scar cannot afford such.
The scar prefers to travel light,
sometimes disguised as pleasure,
or even a special kind of gesture.
Its favorite ride is the exquisitely
designed nerve to the tongue,
which carries it, pollen, across
old understandings, pages, images
and rhymes, from time to time
gathering itself in silence,
refreshing itself with opened flesh.

*

A fear sat in the moonlight,
sad and confused: "I am a fear
of what?" he asked himself.
"Don't I have to be a fear of
something?" He worried he had
never grown up, that he was
only pretending to be an adult
fear. All the other fears seemed
defined, themselves, real.
In the moonlight he remembered
nothing of his origin. "Maybe
if I knew where I came from…."
Men? Women? Fire? Flood?
The dark? The cold? Spiders? Blood?
Who were my mother and father?
He feared the moonlit answer.

*

A war was walking down a road
between two neighborhoods. He
stopped from time to time to give
candy to children on either side.
The children were hungry, and
the candy made them hungrier.
That's the kind of candy it was.
The war liked their little bellies
and their high voices and thin
limbs, and he liked to walk back,
when he had no candy, and listen
to their tiny begging, *please Mr.,*
and how by morning the lovely
green jewels of the flies flashed
swarming on their still-wet eyes.

*

An ear lost the knack of knowing
a threat from a song. A mosquito
(although there was no mosquito)
was busy in it day and night. Loud
noises: explosions, sirens, shouts,
made the little hairs in the ear curl
and shrivel as if burnt. On the train
between the heart and brain the ear
rode, rocking from side to side in
the deafening tunnel, wondering
if *ear is to hear as earth is to hearth*
holds up or is false and useless.
There was a voice, from somewhere,
singing about futility, or maybe
threatening to ring every bell at once.

The Real Earth

Wake, sit, pivot, put
your two feet on the floor.
You can't fly after all.

(Good thing: that wasn't
the real earth
you were falling toward.)

The kettle whistles in the kitchen.
Your love is at the table
with the morning paper,

buttering her toast, already
sighing at the day's
mendacity and folly.

Libera Nos a Malo

1.

A friend halfway around the world
refers to his home as his motherland.
His email asks me to understand,

but half a century in that last century
purged for me some arrangements
of words no matter who deploys them.

Fallout, we call such consequences now.

2.

I have lived here all my life but
never on just earth, rather
on a language landfill, mounded
and overgrown with tinder, dry,
inviting an errant spark, a cigarette
flicked from a fiction headed
elsewhere fast on cruise control.

Residue rumbles away on a signal
via satellite down iron tracks now
overgrown with grasshoppered weeds,
the smell of sun on creosote.

3.

Who dies? Soldiers? Or sons?
Real boys, facedown among
the scattered corpses:

in brown water at the cattle crossing,
wedged in a crevice in the rock,
scattered across a blasted field.

Then blessings, old-school as a last
cracked chunk of Naptha soap,
are chanted over graves (oh man,
hard work, fat city in full view,)

the mourners' full measure of grief
the principal product
of what had once been wilderness.

The age of wonders was one short story.

4.

Here is a riddle: if I am
            a misgiving, tagged in a code
to scan, a son at the sky's edge
            waiting for love or money,
marked man from smoketown,
            a lyric sung at zero dB,
gravity's own voice, perhaps
            a little blue boy of a singular
urge, why was I born and why
            do I feel foolish asking why?

5.

The dead are noisy as a hedge of wrens.
I am ignored among them.

Whose is that face in the shadows?
The art of this inquiry is all night

work, done while weeping for them,
their separate woes, our common lives.

6.

Afterward, forward
is undefined. I suspect the past
does not resemble its photos:

breath in a jar,
tremulous as a willow,

so long see you
a single parenthesis mark
in the long dialogue,

when the grass is straw,
and the ants, the bees, and all
the late languages
are ghosts, each one alone,
bewildered by the music
of creaking branches.

7.

Deaf to the winter sun,
I returned where the grass
would never again be as tall.

Late messenger, the bare trees
whispered, pray for forgiveness.

All of my fathers are dying.
The archive is on fire.

The possible arts: resistance,
refusal, requiem, remembering,

require another schoolroom
where the work, parsing the syntax

of the ways things happen, scars
inadmissible, begins again.

8.

Fixations and saccades:
certain movements of the eyes
are discouraged,

redirected to luminous
ciphers, fixed like a laser
on the heart of the amygdala,

and our children, never
having read a word
of mercy, will be our jurors.

9.

Once I no longer believed,
I could not say what it was
I had believed.
             The words themselves
became delight, illuminating
a single yearning,
                   and I saw that darkness,
reassuring, undescribed, remained.

And I can still see paradise aflame
through all the days of obligation.

The Road

Mothers with newborns in knotted slings,
on their heads impossible towers of things,

    the old in carts, the children by the hand,
    these people crossing a cratered land

        are more than metaphor;
            but they are also metaphor.

We are the truth to one another. Look:
don't wait for some historian's book

    to understand this (then it will be too late.)
    This is the unchecked power of the State,

        the end of empathy, the rise of Mars,
          the avarice that in the end mars

all our laws and medicine and art.
Show me one fleeing person's heart

    and I will show you a thousand griefs
    for loves, hopes, memories, beliefs

        that war has undermined.
          Corpses plowed under, mined

roads and fields, the groves and orchards
poisoned, fathers and brothers tortured,

    hope abandoned with the other heavy furniture —
    it isn't much of a road, the future,

        if you don't know where
          it goes or it goes nowhere.

Arrival

Phnom Penh, Cambodia

ID, visa, passport. I always
hated my face in that picture.
Other countries in red, in history,
none of them the longed-for place

where silence might be peace
again, as it had been long ago
when birds in their chattering
paused to hear what I might sing,

not this other silence, carry-on
in the overhead compartment,
bag of silence in which a man no
longer hears his own heart, doubt

is so strong. Nowhere, I listened
to the engine's roar, black outside.
In the airport, a man with a sign
welcomed me, brought me here

to enmity's aftermath, renewal
clear in your voices, inflections
of my mother tongue so new,
each word was cleaned, polished,

and every word, each magical
translation from Khmer or French
awakened a word in me, until
silence was peace, as it had been

welcoming my voice, back
when birds in their chattering
paused to hear what I might sing,
then answered me with dawn.

Rune

A day nears, feast
of a saint unborn,
unlike our forebears'
or any we have known.

We know how dark
are powers kept in darkness
(a broken lock, a stopped clock,
masks, and lies.)

When we wake
that unexampled day,
will we believe ourselves
free or broken?

Monument

Should there be
a memorial, a stone

inscribed
To Those Who Resisted,

let it not be placed
in the square
renamed so many times,

nor in the park
where the poor seek shelter,

nor the busy plaza.

Should there be
a memorial, build it

deep in a forest,
high on a mountain,

requiring one to be
a pilgrim, perhaps

on a rock in the harbor;
no, in the heart,

yes, in the heart,
a stone in the heart.

Part Four

Longfellow's Heart

Tell me not, in mournful numbers...

Oh we know, we have
mourned, you know, so
no need to go urging
our souls toward your
told-you-so's, their
subtext gaudiam brevis,
believe me, we get it,

we of the sick, rank, dirty
body, donkey body, pig
body, body the colostomy
bag of spirit, rot as lurid
as Breughel's hell, frog
body, offal casing, of course
we want to live forever,

but only with this burning
body, tickle body, body
flushed, delicious, parent
body, child body, belly
button, cock, and lovely
pussy body, body upright,
toes for balance, noses red
in cold, our earlobes soft

to lips, the tongue itself
almost a mind, exhausted
body drinking sleep, old
body full of dreams, good
shoddy body, hungry body,
not fear body, bone body,
not alone, abandoned
in the earth, not that one.

Ghost

I don't know the first thing to say about the dead,
          not even how to begin to think about them. Unsure
               if visitations, in dreams or otherwise, are real or merely
          literary, I don't even know if I should call this hope
or superstition, but I saw you in the Dublin airport

          at the baggage carousel in January, perplexity,
impatience, and anticipation in your gaze
          as you stared at me before I lost you in the crowd.
               It could be that I saw you then because I loved you, or
was starting to — I loved your laugh and miss it, crossing

          at that busy corner between our offices and classrooms —
               it could be only that I needed to acknowledge that.
If you appear again, this time I'll try not to make that noise
          the living make with our breath that's not a word,
               that lets us turn from meaning, shrug, and walk away.

Chimera

Again and again I mistake
the knot on that branch
for a bird, each morning
the same figure emerging
from the linden's chiaroscuro.

Could it be that as the knot
reappears the bird I saw
resumes its duty, welcoming
the newly inanimate dead?
Is that why I have never heard it?

If so, I admire its steadfast perch,
its sublime and silent call
of warning, its patient waiting
for the day when I am not
so easily and fortunately fooled.

Nottigan's Wraith

A metaphor
not allowed
or understood
is a ghost

as glaciers calve
because
that ice, icily
figurative

or that barred view
or stars
stood under

may not
any longer
mean

and fractured ken
and acumen
all at once
is fearsome
wrathful
fact

knock knock/who's there?
Nottigan.

Run! Run and hide.

To See the Elephant Jump the Fence

Like a man in an iron lung or carrying a sax or syringe,
a couple of hundred years from now no one will know
what this thing is that keeps me alive: how will they live?

Goatherds listened to bleating and clanking bells
while they tried to understand what their mariner cousins
told them of parabolic dramas in the starlit heavens:

(They must be crazy — all that rocking on the water does it.
Half the time I think they think we're stupid out here cold
on the mountainside and only mean to frighten us to death.)

But the future consumes us all our lives, like a man eating
chips, and when the bag is empty he will lick his fingers
one by one and crumple it; or a woman scrubbing at a stain;

or a nun praying a rosary; or a girl jumping rope for as long
as she can or is allowed, singing the same song over and over,
reciting what she has learned by heart. Let us be grateful.

Corollary

The body,
six feet
underground,

requires
six days
to break down.

Bulbs must wait
in warming loam
six months

or more. And so
the earth is vast,
love urgent.

Inventory

What I have given to sorrow,
though I have poured out
all I am again and again,
does not amount to much.

One winter's snows.
Two loves I could not welcome.
A year of mostly silence.
Another man I might have been.

Hatteras

Back then, on that thin strip of barrier
island, at your parents' beachfront
house, we were at war with each other
over territory: psychic premises, time,
responsibilities, attention. We plumbed
desire and fury, threatened each other
with abandonment. Sometimes the wind
would shift and blow from inland, across
the sound, not from the sea, and bring
dank pressure and a horde of insects,
tropical, hard and heavy, banging into
the screens, hanging there with barbed legs
and the faces of demons. I snapped them off
with my middle finger, which annoyed you,
sitting across from me under the lamp
that had drawn them to our windows,
nursing our newborn and trying to read.
What did we know about love? Why did
we stay together, we two, grandparents
now, long married, writing books,
our dedications to each other in italics?
The wind would shift, again and again.
We seem to have known at least that much.

for K.

Downpour

Ah, this rain. Now this is the rain
I remember. It has been a long time
since its billion bubbles rattled on
the blackened street and burbled
in the sewer grate where leaves
wadded, since it combed the grass
and washed away dirt to red clay.
I had never given up expecting it,
even when the edges of my thin
desires crinkled and turned brown,
and somehow even when the names
of my dead, midmemory, eluded me,
and I tried not to be angry at myself
for fear I would burst into flames.
Now you can hear the flood below
the streets and sidewalks, power
you feel through the soles of your feet,
and I am drenched again in gladness.

Three Pair of Shoes, Vincent Van Gogh, 1886

Six shoes,
same size.
The toes
on two
agape, and one
I allegorize

turned over
like a glass
refusing wine or
a riderless
horse
behind a hearse.

You see?
You say
"tongue"
and before long
it speaks
what looks,
sorry,
like a story,

it is up to us:
of these shoes,
that odd one posits
a protagonist,

a hero or heroine,
our stand-in.

What Redon Knew

Odilon Redon, 1840-1916

To chain an angel you only need
a frightened animal, to ride a chariot
anemones and poppies;
and if you allow the apparition
(a simple trick of the aurora), it is possible
the pair of figures in the small boat in the foreground
leaning toward each other are talking of the very time
that you are living through right now,
though they are far out on the water.

Or perhaps the chalice was never meant for you,
and all along you were only a knot of fear and yearning,
a thorny wish the world would cooperate, and after
you had closed your eyes a while, look different
enough, for a moment, to compose a vision all your own,
something only nearly true, not true, a comfort, a truce,
a prayer to a god who climbed to invisibility, ascending
like the balloon the child was warned not to let go of,
and not the frightening teeth in the dark,
the chimera, the phantom in the window.

After all, things germinate because a spirit is in them,
whether or not we choose to think we can name it, and because
they are preparing to die. Orpheus was only able
to sing the creatures into harmony, not change their natures.
The well will always have only your undulant face in it,
perplexed and blank as any creature of the sea, or as an old self
you no longer know what to make of, and which certainly
does not know what to make of what's become of you.

The Buddha in his youth was wealthy, gifted, and ignorant
as a man asleep among flowers: the family bonsai, groomed
and twisted, he didn't even know he was in pain. How could he,
kept from anybody else's suffering? Closed eyes, closed eyes,
closed eyes everywhere he looked, but his were opened.

All those years of his blindness a kind of chrysalis,
perfecting his foolishness, protecting his tenderness,
so that, shocked as an infant, pained as a child,
but older, he was able to ask the question
the rest of us, for several thousand years, could not recall.

Eventually we will climb in the red boat with blue sails
because we find it beautiful, no matter if that means righteousness
or calm, adventure or repose, a promise or fulfillment of a promise.
No one has ever yet been able to resist, and you may choose
to believe therefore that no one has ever wanted to.
If you prefer the yellow boat, it will come for you
one day when you discover the wheel of fortune, compared
to flames and flowers, seashells and trees, the faces of the living,
and even silence, is a toy that you, an aged angel, have outgrown.

Notes

"Infant," p. 13: This poem is a rendering of my very rudimentary understanding of mother-infant interpersonal neurobiology and the intergenerational transmission of trauma, based on the work of Dan Siegel, and Francoise Davoine and Jean-Max Gaudillere's *History Beyond Trauma*.

"For a Slain Poet," p. 36: The poet Hashem Shaabani was executed on January 27th, 2014, by the Islamic Republic of Iran for *Moharebeh*, i.e. "waging war on God" and for opposing the republic by promoting Arabic culture.

"Arrival," p. 53: The Second South-South Institute on Sexual Violence Against Men and Boys took place in Phnom Penh, Cambodia, in May 2015. The first Institute took place two years earlier in Kampala, Uganda. In 2017, the Institute will convene in Christchurch, New Zealand. The Institute concerns itself especially with sexual violence against men and boys in war zones, its meaning and consequence.

"Longfellow's Heart," p. 57: The epigraph is from Longfellow's "A Psalm of Life."

"Ghost," p. 58, is in memoriam, Sarah Hannah, 1967-2007.

"To See the Elephant Jump the Fence," p. 61: "To See the Elephant Jump the Fence" is a line from a children's jump-rope chant.

"Downpour," p. 65, is for Saul Touster.

"What Redon Knew," p. 67: Odilon Redon, 1840-1916, was a French Symbolist painter. The poem attempts to animate, via narrative, the images in his catalogue.

Acknowledgments

The author wishes to thank the editors of the following journals, in which some of these poems first appeared, sometimes in earlier versions: *Agni*, *The Breakwater Review*, *Chautauqua*, *Heart Quarterly*, *Ibbetson Street*, *The Manhattan Review*, *Omphalos*, *The Same*, *Sojourners*, and *(Un)civil.*

"On Being Asked to Write a Poem on the Theme of Liberation" and "Rune" were first published in the anthology *Liberation: New Works on Freedom from Internationally Renowned Poets*, ed. Mark Ludwig. Boston. Beacon Press, 2015.

I am grateful to my editor, Peter Covino, for his collegial and critical readings of successive drafts of these poems. I also want to thank Kathleen Aguero, Richard Cambridge, Dennis Nurkse, Saul Touster, and Baron Wormser for their criticism and encouragement.

Love and gratitude to the "soup group": Thom Harrigan, Steve Klarer, Mike Lew, Ellen Silver, and Zoya Slive.

Richard Hoffman is author of six previous books: the poetry collections *Without Paradise*, *Gold Star Road*, and *Emblem*; the memoirs *Love & Fury* and *Half the House*; and the short story collection *Interference and Other Stories*. He is Senior Writer in Residence at Emerson College, in Boston.

BARROW STREET POETRY

A Dangling House
Maeve Kinkhead (2017)

Noon until Night
Richard Hoffman (2017)

Kingdom Come Radio Show
Joni Wallace (2016)

In Which I Play the Runaway
Rochelle Hurt (2016)

Detainee
Miguel Murphy (2016)

The Dear Remote Nearness of You
Danielle Legros George (2016)

Our Emotions Get Carried Away Beyond Us
Danielle Cadena Deulen (2015)

Radioland
Lesley Wheeler (2015)

Tributary
Kevin McLellan (2015)

Horse Medicine
Doug Anderson (2015)

This Version of Earth
Soraya Shalforoosh (2014)

Unions
Alfred Corn (2014)

O, Heart
Claudia Keelan (2014)

Last Psalm at Sea Level
Meg Day (2014)

Vestigial
Page Hill Starzinger (2013)

You Have to Laugh: New + Selected Poems
Mairéad Byrne (2013)

Wreck Me
Sally Ball (2013)

Blight, Blight, Blight, Ray of Hope
Frank Montesonti (2012)

Self-evident
Scott Hightower (2012)

Emblem
Richard Hoffman (2011)

Mechanical Fireflies
Doug Ramspeck (2011)

Warranty in Zulu
Matthew Gavin Frank (2010)

Heterotopia
LesleyWheeler (2010)

This Noisy Egg
NicoleWalker (2010)

Black Leapt In
Chris Forhan (2009)

Boy with Flowers
Ely Shipley (2008)

Gold Star Road
Richard Hoffman (2007)

Hidden Sequel
Stan Sanvel Rubin (2006)

Annus Mirabilis
Sally Ball (2005)

A Hat on the Bed
Christine Scanlon (2004)

Hiatus
Evelyn Reilly (2004)

3.14159+
Lois Hirshkowitz (2004)

Selah
Joshua Corey (2003)